AF201691

# Why Go to Confession?

## Questions and Answers About Sacramental Reconciliation

Rev. Joseph M. Champlin

*Nihil Obstat:*
Rev. Arthur J. Espelage, O.F.M.
Rev. Robert L. Hagedorn

*Imprimi Potest:*
Rev. John Bok, O.F.M., Provincial

*Imprimatur:*
Most Reverend Carl K. Moeddel, V.G.
Archdiocese of Cincinnati
May 31, 1995

The *nihil obstat* and *imprimatur* are a declaration that a book is considered to be free from doctrinal or moral error. It is not implied that those who have granted the *nihil obstat* and *imprimatur* agree with the contents, opinions or statements expressed.

Scripture citations are taken from *The New American Bible With Revised New Testament*, copyright ©1986 by the Confraternity of Christian Doctrine, and are used by permission. All rights reserved.

Cover illustration by Virginia Broderick
Cover and book design by Mary Alfieri
ISBN 0-86716-263-5

Copyright ©1996, Joseph M. Champlin
All rights reserved.

Published by St. Anthony Messenger Press
Printed in the U.S.A.

St. Anthony Messenger Press
AND FRANCISCAN COMMUNICATIONS
Cincinnati, Ohio

# CONTENTS

# Part One:
# **Why Confess Our Sins Anyway?**

### ***Why should we confess our sins?***

A simple analysis of our actions would probably reveal that we basically do certain things for one of two reasons or for a combination of both: Someone tells us we have to do this, or we judge that doing it will somehow benefit us.

Applied to the matter at hand, such an analysis indicates we celebrate the Sacrament of Reconciliation either because God and the Church command us to do so or because we see some value in it.

Those two motivations, however, actually bear a close relationship to each other. The connection may not appear immediately, but in the end what the Lord and Christ's Church mandate for us will, when carried out, promote our best interests, lead to our deeper happiness and simultaneously facilitate the well being of all others.

Thus, while the Catholic Church does require members to confess their sins and receive the Sacrament of Penance or Reconciliation, those who comply with that directive will discover that the action also produces for them significant psychological, social and spiritual benefits.

We will begin this booklet by explaining some of those beneficial results from sacramental reconciliation: the removal of sin and guilt and the growth in grace and virtue.

# Sin and Guilt

### *What do people mean by the word* **guilt** *or the phrase "feeling guilty"?*

I have no clear answer to that question. Persons today use this term to describe a variety of situations in which they feel uncomfortable, awkward, chagrined or ashamed. In many cases those individuals were not at all responsible for the action that led to the unpleasant state or feeling labeled "guilt" or "guilty."

For example, a man dying of cancer discovered that the effects of the disease had left him with no control over his intestinal system. He frequently became incontinent and soiled the bedclothes with all the unpleasantness and feelings of shame that tend to accompany such an accident. In the midst of that discomfort and embarrassment, he said in anguish to a friend, "I feel very guilty about this, causing you and the others so much inconvenience and work."

"Feeling guilty" described for him his distressful situation. Yet he was guilty of no moral fault, had committed no sin and could not in any way be held responsible for the troublesome event.

Such confusion about the word *guilt*, so common in today's society, makes it essential that we start with clear and relatively precise definitions.

### *How do you define sin and guilt?*

Sin and guilt, like all ultimate realities of life, actually defy precise definitions. We can thus provide only general descriptions of both terms.

Sin occurs when we fail to heed the divine imperative within us. God in our heart tells us to do this and we don't do it. God in our heart tells us not to do something, yet we go ahead and do it.

Guilt is the objective state which follows from this failure to follow our conscience, the divine inner imperative, God's directing voice within our hearts. As a result of sin [illegible] guilt.

AF570730

## *Have we lost a sense of sin?*

Some religious leaders and mental health experts maintain that, for various reasons, during the past half century many have lost a healthy sense of sin.

This is regrettable because without a proper appreciation of sinfulness we see no need for repentance and forgiveness, no need for a sacrament of mercy, no need for a Church which proclaims the Good News of God's constant willingness to forgive and, ultimately, no need for Jesus, the Savior who frees us from sin and guilt.

## *Are there different kinds of guilt?*

Yes. For the sake of clarity, we can say there are two basic types: true and false guilt.

True guilt is objective, rational and based on fact. It exists when we actually do something we know to be wrong or fail to carry out some good deed that in our judgment we had been called to perform. We have sinned and are guilty.

False guilt is subjective, irrational and based on fantasy. It exists when we inaccurately blame ourselves for some deed, or continue to punish ourselves for past misdeeds. In such situations, we either did not sin at all or not as severely as we judge, or we have long since been forgiven and yet still carry the oppressive burden of guilt.

### ✚ *Would you explain in more detail the meaning of false guilt?*

Gladly, because in today's world many bear, unnecessarily, the painful and permeating affliction of false guilt.

Here are some of the more common kinds of false guilt:

**1) *Making moral molehills into mortal sin mountains.*** Persons with this tendency judge that minor character flaws or venial, lesser sins are major, mortal failures that break our friendship with God. They exaggerate the degree of evil present and allow that distortion to rob them of serenity or peace.

To confess missing prayers on one morning and to abstain from Communion because of that omission could be an illustration of this tendency.

**2) *Never letting go of forgiven sins.*** We need always to stand before God as sinners requiring grace and salvation. We also can benefit from an awareness of past misdeeds; such a consciousness may enhance a healthy humility and sharpen our sensitivity in dealing with others' human frailty. But worrying about whether sins have actually been forgiven, becoming obsessed with past misdeeds and not allowing God's mercy previously bestowed in confession to liberate us from those faults cripple a person.

**3) *Blaming ourselves for events beyond our control or responsibility.*** This inaccurate blaming and the false guilt which flows from it often center around accidents, parent-child relationships, sickness, old age and death.

- A classmate of mine one year out of high school was driving home in the early summer twilight when a young child dashed out from the grassy, country roadside into the path of her car. The youngster died instantly. My friend had to deal with heavy guilt feelings for years even though she was totally free of blame for the tragic accident.

- Parents question and blame themselves when children develop an addiction to alcohol or other drugs, drop out of school, become pregnant outside of marriage, run afoul of the law, cease attending church or otherwise falter and fail to follow the course pointed out by Mom and Dad. Mothers and fathers subsequently torture themselves with self-doubts. They experience deep guilt even though objective outsiders would testify that their parenting was informed and conscientious.

- Grown-up children wrestle with guilt about not visiting parents often enough or placing feeble ones in nursing homes. Adults also may torture themselves afterward for failing to have detected suicidal signs or for being physically absent at the moment of death.

Sacramental reconciliation can sometimes help with these cases of false guilt. It may aid in correcting an erroneous conscience, reassure an especially sensitive sinner and clarify the vision of an excessively questioning individual. But false guilt normally requires healing more than forgiveness, and sometimes professional therapy as well as the priest's proclamation of God's loving mercy.

## *Is there any difference between being guilty and feeling guilty?*

Being and feeling guilty are not necessarily identical. A person may actually be quite guilty and yet not experience any guilt feelings. On the other hand, as we noted above, some persons feel very guilty, but in fact are not guilty of a misdeed at all.

The state of being guilty may overflow into feelings of guilt, but not automatically. Nor does the intensity of guilt feelings serve as an accurate measure of the evil for which we are responsible. We tend to experience stronger guilt feelings for sins of human passion (sexual faults, intemperance, unjust or improper anger) than for less physical sins (pride, uncharitableness, injustice). Those latter failures, however, very likely are more harmful than the former faults.

## *Does the difference between being and feeling guilty apply to being forgiven and feeling forgiven?*

Absolutely. Penitents often walk out of a reconciliation room feeling liberated, joyful and at peace; but sometimes they experience no particularly strong feelings of elation or relief. Still, if people carry truly repentant hearts to the Sacrament of Penance, they will always leave with sins forgiven.

## *What specific help does the Church offer for healing and forgiveness?*

The *Catechism of the Catholic Church* (see #1420-1422) specifically categorizes the Sacrament of Penance or Reconciliation as one of two “sacraments of healing.” (The other is Anointing of the Sick.) Just as Christ forgave the sins of the paralytic and restored him to bodily health, so Jesus through the Church continues today his work of healing and salvation.

Only God can forgive the real guilt carried by our sins. The Lord does this most effectively through the Sacrament of Penance. But God also wishes to heal the other effects of sins as well as the painful suffering brought on by false guilt. The Lord accomplishes this in many ways, including the Sacrament of Anointing.

### *How will confessing to the priest help me with the problem of guilt?*

Moral guilt arises within us when some wrong we have done or some good we have failed to do breaks or weakens our relationship with God, with each other, with the world around us and with our inner selves. This condition may spill over into our feelings, leaving us filled with remorse and discouragement.

When we approach the priest and confess our sins with sincere hearts, those broken or weakened relationships are restored or strengthened. The God Scripture describes as slow to be angry and swift to forgive embraces us, welcomes us back home and washes away in the blood of Christ our guilt and sinfulness. We are reunited with our sisters and brothers. Our inner self once again becomes whole and healthy.

Pope John Paul II, in his encyclical *Reconciliation and Penance*, states that reconciliation with God leads to reconciliations of other rifts caused by sin. Forgiven penitents are reconciled with themselves in their inmost being where they regain their innermost truth. They are reconciled with their neighbors whom they have in some way offended and wounded. They are reconciled with the

Church. They are reconciled with all creation.

Frequently we feel clean, uplifted and forgiven; but more important, we *are* clean, uplifted and forgiven. God has indeed pardoned us.

## ✚ *Is this the only way I can be rid of my guilt?*

An impressive array of psychiatrists, psychologists and counselors testify that without some admission of sin a person will lack deep interior peace and may suffer intense inner turmoil.

One spiritual writer, noting that people sometimes seek to repress or deny real guilt, observes: "The consequences of repression are not long delayed.... The disturbing element, temporarily stifled, continues to exert its influence from the depth of the unconscious.... The repressed element poisons human life and throws it out of gear, reintroducing itself in the form of new and ultimately irrepressible kinds of distress."[1]

Another analyst comments: "Increasingly it appears that the central fact in personality disorder is real guilt and that it can be radically resolved only by confession that has at least a quasi-public character."[2]

Contemporary novels, plays and movies occasionally dramatize the point that unacknowledged and unexpiated guilt is perhaps the greatest source of personal anxiety or inner pain.

For example, in one novel a Gentile girl, burdened by an incident of premarital sex, wishes to "confess" this lapse to a Jewish rabbi. He is reluctant to listen to her tale, but she insists: "Yes, don't you see, I haven't been able to tell anybody.... I apologize.... I've always wanted to tell somebody about that ever since it happened. I grew so disgusted with myself afterwards...."[3]

## *Why confess to a priest? Why not to a friend, an adviser or a community of people?*

Psychoanalyst Erich Fromm, who is not Roman Catholic, nevertheless judges that the Catholic Church has "more adequate means" for dealing with a sense of guilt than other religions and institutions.[4] Here are a few reasons why that may be true:

- The priest charges no fee. He freely received from God the power to declare sins forgiven in Jesus' name and thus must freely exercise for others that ministry of mercy.
- The priest strictly keeps confidences learned in the reconciliation chapel. Church laws governing what we term "the seal of confession" under severest penalty prohibit a priest from revealing any sin of an individual penitent to any person under any conditions. The long history of this sacrament indicates that priests, despite their human weaknesses in other areas, have nevertheless observed those restrictions remarkably well. Confessors take these rules very, very seriously.
- The priest's wide experience, acquired through regularly hearing many confessions, gives him deep insights into human guilt and divine mercy.
- The priest pronounces with authority and in an audible voice God's forgiveness of sins:

> "...[T]hrough the ministry of the Church may God give you pardon and peace, and I absolve you from your sins in the name of the Father, and of the Son, and of the Holy Spirit."[5]

People walk away from the Sacrament of Penance having actually heard these clear and certain words of liberation. They know guilt is gone and sins are removed. Friends, advisers and others can comfort or reassure on this matter, but not announce with such certitude.

- The priest carries out the promises of Christ. After the resurrection, Jesus said to his disciples: "Receive the Holy Spirit. Whose sins you forgive are forgiven them, and whose sins you retain are retained" (John 20:22b-23).
- The priest seeks to mirror in his attitude, words and actions the gentleness of Christ. There are over a dozen incidents in the Gospels which either describe Jesus actually forgiving a repentant sinner or teaching about God's mercy, which has no limit and lasts forever. The Savior's example serves as a role model for priests in the sacrament.
- The priest and the penitent actually celebrate a sacrament, the Sacrament of Penance or Reconciliation. Confession of sins with absolution is more than a merely human ritual that cleanses away unpleasant guilt. As one of the seven sacraments established by Christ, Penance not only forgives sins, but also restores or increases sanctifying grace. Moreover, Reconciliation bestows actual graces that heal the wounds caused by our sins and strengthen the virtues needed for our progress.
- The priest in the name of the Church reconciles us with the community. Sin, as we have seen, weakens or ruptures our relationships with God, others and the world around us. In this sacrament, the priest both declares that those fractured relationships have been restored and aids in rebuilding them.

## ***Does the Church then say I must confess my sins to a priest?***

Yes and no. Serious, grave or mortal sins must be confessed

to a priest; venial sins need not be confessed, though it can be very helpful to do so.

The Church, true enough, obliges us to confess only serious sin, but encourages us to confess venial sins as well, knowing that the confession of sin and reception of the sacrament will bring enormous benefits to the sincere penitent.

In the words of the *Catechism*, "Without being strictly necessary, confession of everyday faults (venial sins) is nevertheless strongly recommended by the Church" (#1458).

The confession of sin in the Sacrament of Penance or Reconciliation also can help us grow in grace and develop different virtues. In the next section, we will describe how it accomplishes those results.

## Grace and Virtue

### ✠ *Since I have not committed any serious fault and do not feel burdened with guilt, why should I confess trivial sins and small transgressions?*

The revised rite of Penance offers this answer to that question: "...[T]hose who through daily weakness fall into venial sins draw strength from a repeated celebration of penance to gain the full freedom of the children of God...to conform more closely to Christ and to follow the voice of the Spirit more attentively."[6]

The *Catechism of the Catholic Church* expands on those words. It teaches that regular confession of venial sins helps us form our conscience and fight against evil tendencies. The practice also enables us to be healed by Christ and to progress in the life of the Spirit. By receiving more frequently through this sacrament the gift of God the Father's mercy, we are motivated to be merciful as God is merciful (see #1458).

### *How, practically speaking, will confession of my minor sins make me fully free, closer to Christ, open to the Spirit and more loving toward my neighbor?*

Here are a few ways in which the Sacrament of Penance does that:

- As a sacrament, it restores or increases sanctifying grace, the life of the risen Christ within us.
- The sacrament also communicates actual graces, God-given insights and strengths to overcome specific faults and deepen particular virtues.
- In the words of a parishioner, "Penance is a time to talk over a problem we might be having with ourselves, our neighbors or relatives." The priest with his training, experience and grace of Holy Orders can be a wise and supportive guide in that regard, although ongoing and lengthy counseling should take place outside the sacrament.
- Regular celebrations of this type enable us to take more honest looks at ourselves and push us to work harder at overcoming our faults.
- Through these careful, prayerful celebrations of reconciliation we perform an act of humility, publicly acknowledge our faith, express our need for forgiveness and sensitize our conscience to the wider dimensions of sinfulness.

## Are you saying my sins can only be forgiven through this sacrament?

Not at all. The Church has always taught that an act of perfect contrition, an expression of sorrow for sin made from the pure love for God, expressed directly to God can secure forgiveness of any sin, including serious or mortal faults. Moreover, venial sins may be forgiven in a variety of ways; e.g., through prayer, works of charity, reading of Scripture and devout reception of the Eucharist.

Church regulations require the confession of serious sin and urge the frequent confession of venial faults for the reasons noted above. But they also strongly encourage acts of perfect contrition and those good deeds which have the power to remit sin.

## How often, then, should I receive the Sacrament of Penance?

An alienated Catholic, who has broken her or his relationship with God, should seek out peace as soon as possible. Catholics who have been walking faithfully with the Lord ought to receive the sacrament as often as they find it helpful for their spiritual growth. No exact time guideline can be given for that—so unique are we as persons—but the move over the past decade from weekly or monthly to yearly or even less frequent confession seems an unhealthy development.

One respected theologian maintains that those truly concerned about their interior lives will confess at least once a month. Another recommends ordinary parishioners approach Penance about four times a year—like the old Ember Days, around Christmas, Easter, the end of school and the beginning of fall.

### ***Since my confessions tend to include the same sins and not be much different from those made when I was in grammar school, do you have any suggestions for changing them into more adult and realistic expressions of my shortcomings?***

As we have observed, serious sins need to be mentioned explicitly and specifically. However, if there has been no mortal or radical break with the Lord, we are free to include or omit whatever we wish.

Some spiritual writers and teachers today urge us to look at our general attitudes and predominant weaknesses in addition to specific actions when preparing for the sacrament. Examining the general sweep of our lives and any attitudes which require change or improvement may prove a more helpful approach than a mere listing of sins.

For example, it is one thing to confess: "I was angry and irritable a certain number of times." It is another to confess: "I am facing surgery soon to remove a growth and have felt worried, nervous and edgy. As a result I have lost my temper with the family and become upset out of proportion over things which went wrong at home."

The latter approach reveals much more and gets to the root of the issue. In addition, it aids both penitent and priest in their discussion about how to deal with the anger and irritation.

### ***Would you develop that a bit more?***

When persons with no conscious serious sin prepare for Reconciliation, they might, instead of drawing up a list of venial faults and straining to approximate the number of times they committed these failings, take a broad, sweeping glance at the past few weeks or months. In this sweep, they would search for the sinful or evil attitudes behind the actions rather than concentrate on the external deeds themselves.

Several guides could be useful in making that examination of conscience or review of one's life:

- Comparing one's life with the virtues, Beatitudes or commandments is one method.
- Reflecting on God's words which command us to love the Lord with our whole heart, to love our neighbor as ourself and to be perfect as our heavenly Father is perfect is another.
- Asking oneself these questions, "What have I done?" "Why did I do it?" "How can I be better?" is still another.
- Looking at our relationships with God, others, the world around us and ourselves is even another.

## *Isn't sin a matter between God and me? Why all this talk about relationships?*

The effect of sinfulness extends beyond our relationship with God. It weakens or severs our relationships with others as well.

The story of Adam, Eve and their fall in Genesis dramatizes these many dimensions or effects of sinfulness.

Before the fall or "original sin," they were friends with God, comfortable in the Lord's presence; their destiny was to be helpmates for each other; they lived in a garden of paradise; they enjoyed an inner wholeness and peace.

After the fall they hid from God's presence, blamed each other, found the garden and the world no longer so blissful and felt shame within their hearts.

Our sinfulness has the same negative effects. The Sacrament of Reconciliation counters those and enables us to regain our friendship with the Lord, to restore relationships with others, to renew the world around us and to recapture an inner serenity free of guilt.

## ✚ *Are there sins which, strictly speaking, could be termed "social sins"?*

Yes and no. All sin is personal or individual. But personal and individual sins can give rise to situations, structures and institutions which run contrary to God's plan and harm others. We sometimes call them "structures of sin." They express and result from personal sins. These sinful situations subsequently lead others to commit evil actions in turn. Thus in an analogous way we might label those situations, structures and institutions "social sin."

The old system of apartheid in South Africa would be one example. Another illustration could cite a corporation which continues to pollute the environment because of its unwillingness to expend the funds necessary to correct the problem. State funding of abortions might be still another example.

## ✚ *Could you provide some additional contemporary moral concerns covered in the* Catechism*?*

There are many: for instance, euthanasia and the right to die, proper care of animals, the death penalty, homosexual activity, gambling, confidentiality and professional secrets, cohabitation, conscientious objection and Sunday Mass attendance.

## ✠ *What should be my overall attitude before, during and after receiving this sacrament?*

A mix of humility and trust with gratitude and joy. The liberating experience of forgiveness should simultaneously prompt sentiments of deep gratitude and joy within us.

Psalm 32 captures these attitudes:

> As long as I kept silent, my bones wasted away;
> I groaned all the day.
> For day and night your hand was heavy upon me;
> my strength withered as in dry summer heat.
> Then I declared my sin to you;
> my guilt I did not hide.
> I said, "I confess my faults to the LORD,"
> and you took away the guilt of my sin....
> You are my shelter; from distress you keep me;
> with safety you ring me round....
> Be glad in the LORD and rejoice, you just;
> exult, all you upright of heart.
>
> (Psalm 32:3-5, 7, 11)

That mix, which is the way to Christian peace, implies a certain tension: We humbly confess to God that we have been and remain sinners while at the same time we put our unreserved trust in Jesus, who continuously bestows his grace and mercy upon us.

The philosopher Blaise Pascal years ago in his *Pensées* summarized that healthy balance between an awareness of our profound sinfulness and a consciousness of God's merciful love:

> One day a man told me that he was filled with joy and trust when he left the confessional. Another told me that he remained a prey to fear. This made me think that the two of them together would have made one good man, and that each lacked something insofar as he did not possess the feeling of the other.[7]

Part Two:

# How Do We Celebrate Reconciliation Today?

## *Why don't we use the term* confession *anymore?*

We do today more often call this sacrament Penance or Reconciliation. Nevertheless, many still refer to the ritual as confession even though the word does not adequately or fully convey the meaning of the sacrament.

Mentioning our sins to the priest (confession) makes up only part of the rite and, while a normally required ingredient, is not the most important component. True sorrow for our failures and a change of heart are the essential aspects; faith in God's loving mercy, words of advice, absolution by the priest and the healing of relationships form equally vital portions of the ritual.

The word *penance* comes from Latin and Greek roots which mean conversion or a change of heart. It recalls the message of Jesus' first sermon recorded in Mark's account, "Repent, and believe in the gospel" (Mark l:15c). The phrase *Sacrament of Penance* reminds us that reform, conversion or change of heart is the absolutely indispensable requirement for forgiveness of our sins.

### *Why is it also called the Sacrament or Rite of Reconciliation?*

The word *reconciliation* emphasizes that this sacrament seeks to heal relationships with God, others, ourselves and the world around us that have been bruised or broken by sinfulness.

### *Do penitents follow the same procedure as they did in the past when receiving the sacrament, or is everything new and different?*

Some elements are the same; a few, new and different. In the past we confessed our sins, accepted a penance, recited an act of contrition and received absolution from the priest. These continue in the revised Rite of Penance.

The Church, however, in an attempt to make the sacrament a richer experience, has slightly altered the format and provides a wide choice for prayer, readings and acts of sorrow or contrition

### *What is the format like?*

The new yet old character of this ritual should become clear as you read through this basic outline for the revised Rite of Penance:

**1**) The priest welcomes the penitent.

**2**) Both make the Sign of the Cross.

**3**) The priest prays for the penitent who, at the end, answers: "Amen."

**4**) A passage from Scripture is read.

**5**) The penitent confesses his or her sins; the priest discusses the penitent's spiritual state and assigns an act of penance or satisfaction.

**6)** The penitent expresses sorrow by reciting either the traditional formula, one of the ten new prayers provided or similar personal, spontaneous words of contrition.

**7)** When the person has completed her or his act of contrition, the priest extends his hands over the penitent's head (or at least extends his right hand) and pronounces words of absolution.

**8)** The penitent listens prayerfully and, at the conclusion, responds: "Amen."

**9)** The priest says: "Give thanks to the Lord, for he is good."

**10)** The penitent concludes: "His mercy endures forever."

**11)** The priest dismisses the penitent with a prayer or suitable phrase and the penitent responds: "Amen" or "Thank you."

## ✠ *If I forget these steps or do not remember the prayers, what then?*

The priest will gladly assist you. Remember that the Sacrament of Penance is essentially concerned with the heart, not the ritual, with our inner dispositions, not our outward expression of those sentiments.

## ✠ *Where have the confessional boxes gone? What are these so-called rooms of reconciliation? Must I now go face-to-face?*

Our American bishops, in carrying out the directives for the revised Rite of Penance, have encouraged parishes where possible to provide reconciliation rooms or small chapels in which penitents may choose to seek sacramental reconciliation through an informal face-to-face exchange with the priest. The option of kneeling at a fixed confessional screen, which allows for the penitent's anonymity, must also be provided. In every case the freedom of the penitent is to be respected.

With a model reconciliation room, the penitent, for the reasons listed below, actually enjoys more freedom and privacy than in the former "box" or "booth."

- The penitent closes the door and then selects either option—sitting face-to-face, or kneeling or sitting behind the screen. No one outside knows the choice made.
- The penitent can speak in a more normal tone of voice without fear of being overheard.
- A penitent who is in any way disabled (hard of hearing, confined to a wheelchair, blind, unable to kneel) will find the reconciliation chapel more accessible.
- The penitent in the face-to-face or open approach may easily share the Scriptures with the priest and talk readily and in a more relaxed manner about her or his spiritual condition.
- The penitent will experience in the appropriately designed and suitably furnished reconciliation room an atmosphere which speaks of warmth, forgiveness and peace.
- A further benefit of the carefully designed reconciliation room is the opportunity it offers for the priest more visibly to extend his right hand toward the penitent or to extend his hands over the penitent's head as he pronounces the words of absolution.

### *Why does the priest extend his hands over the penitent's head?*

In the early Christian days, sinners were reconciled to the Church in a somewhat similar way. The bishop or his delegate, the priest, indicated the sinner had been received back into the Church by imposing hands upon the penitent Christian.

That gesture of the laying on of hands, mentioned often in the Scriptures, predates Jesus' ministry and was a common ritual gesture even outside the Jewish tradition. It symbolizes, among other things, the consecration of a person, the bestowal of power, the reconciliation of a sinner or the welcoming of a Christian, as well as the outpouring of God's grace and Spirit.

This extension of hands in the Sacrament of Penance can be a very moving experience, a tangible gesture expressive of God's mercy, forgiving and healing us here and now.

### *Must I read the Bible during the Rite of Reconciliation?*

No. In a reconciliation room setting and particularly in the face-to-face arrangement, the priest may invite a penitent to read a section from Scripture or he may read the text himself.

Either way, hearing the biblical passage is meant to stir our faith, enlighten our conscience, strengthen our hope in the limitless love God has for us and help us recognize the merciful Christ in the sacrament.

## *Do I still say an act of contrition? When? With what words?*

Roman Catholics have been making acts of contrition for years. But in the recent past this expression of sorrow for sins during confession has had a varied history. Many of us grew up with the practice of mumbling, "O my God, I am heartily sorry," while the priest pronounced the words of absolution in Latin. Since most did not understand the Latin phrases he proclaimed, it made little difference whether we heard or listened to them.

When the formula for absolution was changed into the vernacular, we began instead to listen to those words, "I absolve you from your sins...." The act of contrition, we were told, should be said by ourselves beforehand.

With the new Rite of Penance, we now make a slight shift. The Church wishes us to express our sorrow within the confession itself. The priest, however, is to wait until we do so, then pronounce the formula of forgiveness in our own language. We say "Amen" after he finishes.

What words of contrition or sorrow do we use? The old "O my God" is fine. A few words of your own are also perfectly acceptable. For those who wish a fresh start, some variety or a little help, the revised rite provides ten different acts of contrition from which you may choose. If you confess in the reconciliation room, you could even read one of those texts.

## *Should children still memorize an act of contrition?*

In my judgment, yes. I encourage young people to memorize one of the ten official formulas so that it can stay with them in the years ahead. Daily repetition of such a prayer should deepen and perfect the inner attitude of sorrow we as Christians ought to have constantly in our hearts.

### Does the priest also use different words in giving absolution?

He employs a new formula which is somewhat similar to the older absolution, but a bit distinct from it. The revised text teaches us that the risen Jesus working in the Holy Spirit through the ministry of the Church reconciles us with the Father, with one another and the world around us. Our "Amen" at the end indicates we believe this.

### Will the priest still give me a penance for my sins?

Yes, but he may seek to discover with you a penance that connects with your confession, one that will help heal the wounds in your heart and assist in overcoming the faults you have mentioned.

The Church today, as in the past, sees the desirability of creative and personal penances in place of or as a complement to the traditional Our Father's and Hail Mary's. It seeks acts of satisfaction which bear a close link with the sins confessed and can thus carry over into the penitent's future life.

Here are a few illustrations:

- Reading an appropriate Scripture passage on trust in God or in the Lord's healing power as a follow-up to the confession of my edginess in the face of surgery.
- Mentioning good points about a person you have criticized.

- Denying yourself something once in response to a sin of intemperance.
- Praying for a person who, through some hurt, has caused you to harbor revengeful, bitter thoughts.

### *Are there any printed materials to help me with a confession according to this new way and also enable me to take a broader view in examining my heart?*

Yes. Some parishes provide cards or books outlining the ritual and containing the texts we have mentioned. A companion booklet, *Meeting the Merciful Christ*,[8] features a simple, scripturally rich, several-step process for the preparation and celebration of Penance. Most Catholic gift or book shops have these and similar publications.

Please recall, however, the earlier response: The Sacrament of Penance is essentially concerned with the heart, not the ritual; with the inner dispositions, not our outward expression of those sentiments.

### *What are these "communal" penance services announced every now and then in our parish?*

Since our sinfulness affects our sisters and brothers, diminishing or destroying relationships with them, the Church wishes to underscore the truth that the Sacrament of Penance presupposes and brings about a reconciliation of people who are alienated. Celebrations of penance which draw a group of people together for common song, prayer, readings, examination of conscience, expressions of sorrow, gestures of peace and blessing help us grasp those points.

Such communal penance services are normally scheduled during Advent and Lent, but also may be arranged at other times.

### ✚ *In these services may we receive absolution without confession?*

Not under ordinary circumstances. Serious sins must be mentioned to the priest, and these celebrations should provide an opportunity for such a disclosure.

General absolution without confession of sins is reserved for extraordinary occasions and even then serious faults, while forgiven, must be mentioned later when the first opportunity for the Sacrament of Penance arises.

### ✚ *If a person has been really terrible, broken all the commandments, committed every sin in the book, been away from Church for years and forgotten what to say or do, is there hope for that individual?*

Absolutely. Listen to these typical statements from Jesus:

> "I tell you,...there will be more joy in heaven over one sinner who repents than over ninety-nine righteous people who have no need of repentance." (Luke 15:7b)

> "For the Son of Man has come to seek and to save what was lost." (Luke 19:10)

Those words indicate our Lord wants to save, forgive and heal us more than we ourselves want to be saved, forgiven, healed.

### ✠ *What does that kind of troubled, confused person say to the priest?*

An easy question. "Father, I have been away from God for a long, long time and want to come back. Will you help me?"

The priest will then gently assist this penitent and in a few brief moments dissolve those heavy burdens, fill the heart with Christ's grace, reconcile that individual to the entire Church, that is, to all her or his brothers and sisters in the Lord, and joyfully welcome the liberated sinner home to a place of peace.

### ✠ *But what if I slip back, stumble or seem stuck with a particular sin?*

Simply return to the sacrament once more, be forgiven and healed, then start over again. As long as at this moment, in this experience of Penance, during this Rite of Reconciliation, you are repentant and wish to change your life, God's mercy and helping graces will flood your heart. What happens afterwards, success or failure, certainly should be related to and affected by the present confession, but is a different matter. All the Lord asks in the sacrament is, "Right here and now, do you love me?"

### ✠ *What should I do if I am reluctant to confess because in the past a priest didn't seem to understand my situation, upset me or even refused absolution?*

Those are regrettable experiences, often leaving deep scars, real hurts and sometimes a reluctance ever to approach the sacrament again. However, while priests strive to imitate the gentle mercy of their Master, they, like you, are human, frail, error-prone vessels of clay; they, like you, can fail; they, like you, can have bad days, make mistakes and injure others.

The Church says to you: Try once more. Go to another priest for penance. Seek out a confessor with whom you are comfortable and who brings you peace. Remember, however, that sometimes good advice can mean bad news. The most saintly, kind and understanding priest may still challenge your life-style or require a change that will be difficult.

### *Does the sacrament really work in all these wonderful ways or are you, the priest, merely trying to convince me?*

Listen to these two testimonies (we could give countless others) and make your own judgment:

A teenager succinctly and plainly comments: "You feel good when you're done with Reconciliation. Now you can start out clean."

A married woman and mother, two decades older than this teenager, writes: "After returning to Penance for the first time in twelve years, I feel so clean, so whole and so loved that I can only ask: Why did I wait so long, endure so much sorrow and suffering when the Lord was there all the time?"

Those are but the modern-day versions of the incident in which Jesus said about the woman known in town as a sinner: "So I tell you, her many sins have been forgiven because she has shown great love...." He then said to her, "Your sins are forgiven.... Your faith has saved you; go in peace" (see Luke 7:36-50).

## Notes

[1] Arnold Uleyn, *Is It I, Lord?* (New York: Holt, Rinehart and Winston, 1969), p. 145.

[2] Donald De Marco, "The Decline of Private Guilt and the Need for Confession," *Emmanuel*, February, 1981, pp. 99-106.

[3] Noah Gordon, *The Rabbi* (New York: Fawcett World Library, 1965), pp. 178-79.

[4] De Marco, op. cit.

[5] *Rite of Penance*, #7a.

[6] *Rite of Penance*, #7b.

[7] Uleyn, op. cit., p. 44.

[8] Rev. Joseph M. Champlin, *Meeting the Merciful Christ* (Cincinnati: St. Anthony Messenger Press and Franciscan Communications, 1989).

# WHY GO TO CONFESSION?

## Questions and Answers About Sacramental Reconciliation

Two practical questions face contemporary Catholics: "Why should we confess our sins?" and "How do we celebrate reconciliation today?" In this booklet Rev. Joseph M. Champlin answers those questions. He explains the beneficial results from sacramental reconciliation: the removal of sin and guilt and the growth in grace and virtue.

**Rev. Joseph M. Champlin**, a priest of the Diocese of Syracuse for forty years, serves now as rector of its cathedral. He has traveled more than a million miles lecturing here and abroad on pastoral subjects and has also written forty books on a variety of Church topics. His latest books are *The Visionary Leader* and *With Hearts Light as Feathers: The Sacrament of First Reconciliation for Children* (Crossroad) and *A Thoughtful Word, A Healing Touch* (Twenty-Third Publications). His illustrated book, *What It Means to Be Catholic* (St. Anthony Messenger Press/Franciscan Communications) is a best-seller.

St. Anthony Messenger Press
AND FRANCISCAN COMMUNICATIONS
1615 Republic St.
Cincinnati, Ohio 45210-1298
(513) 241-5615

$1.95

ISBN 0-86716-263-5
50195
9 780867 162639